THE LANGUAGE OF INFLUENCE AND PERSONAL POWER

{ 316 Insights *for* Life *and* Leading }

SCOTT HAGAN

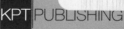
KPT PUBLISHING

The Language of Influence and Personal Power

© 2019 KPT Publishing, LLC
Written by Scott Hagan

Published by KPT Publishing
Minneapolis, Minnesota 55406
www.KPTPublishing.com

ISBN 978-1-944833-56-5

Designed by Koechel Peterson & Associates

First printing January 2019
10 9 8 7 6 5 4 3 2 1

Printed in the United States of America

How to get the most out of this book

WEEKLY TEAM EXERCISE

The recommended size for this exercise is 4 to 15 people.

Have a different team member lead the discussion each week by following the template below. Let the rotation continue until each person has had a turn (ex: If you have 4 team members, do this exercise for four weeks; 8 team members goes for 8 weeks).

- Choose one of the statements that stood out to you and read it to the group.

- Give a brief explanation of why it stood out and how it spoke to you.

Handpick 3-5 of the questions from the list below and present them to the team for group discussion:

1. How does this speak to you when you hear it?

2. Can you think of a leader or person who has embodied this maxim in their life?

3. Is this principle counter-intuitive to your instincts, emotions and/or patterns of thinking? If yes, explain.

4. What are the potential negative consequences of neglecting or ignoring this statement?

5. In your area(s) of responsibility, how can living out this concept improve your influence and effectiveness?

6. How would our team benefit if all of us modeled this value as we worked together?

> **"**
> Great leaders
> see everyone
> in the room.
> Poor leaders only
> notice those who
> notice them.
> **"**

If you think for too long about a missed opportunity, chances are you will miss the next one too.

Nobody's success is robbing
your potential. There's plenty of
wind in the harbor to sail
more than one ship.

**The purpose of
memories is to keep you grateful.**

Anytime you help another person
stay emotionally organized you have
served them well as a friend.

Most vision starts in the form of
shapes and shadows, not clean details.
So, don't be in a rush to describe it.

~

A leader's heart must stay hot.
Once it becomes room temperature,
influence ceases.

The irony of masks is that we wear them to appear strong, yet people are drawn to us when we take them off.

How you describe someone
when they're not around tells
me more about you than
it does about them.

**Whatever you neglect
will deteriorate.**

> You cannot hide your heart. Whatever fills, spills.

Great leaders turn mistakes into information.

When someone looks forward to meeting you, make the experience exceed the rumor.

~

A leader must produce more than they consume.

~

Nothing cures apathy like a good crisis.

~

Never punish the next person because of the actions of the previous person. Each relationship is a clean slate.

"The greatest
gift in life

is to be free of your secrets. "

The best thing about climbing
mountains is that you cannot fake
your way to the top.

**Excess is not success.
True leaders live more moderate
than privileged.**

Don't let a new friend take the place of an old friend. Have two friends.

"

You will never grow
until you first learn how
to protect the progress
you've already made.

"

Momentum doesn't require something monumental. Approach your next inch with passion and you'll be fine.

Actions speak louder than words, especially when you're a hypocrite.

The art of teamwork is knowing how
to sharpen the countenance of
your teammates.

~

**Correct the person ...
just don't insult them.**

~

Jealousy isn't directed
at the success; it's usually
directed at the person.

Lead strategically.
Love spontaneously.

~

We learn far more in
life from the word "no"
than we do from the
word "yes."

We imitate who we admire.
So be careful who you admire.

If you've got it, give it.

You want your protégé
to exceed your accomplishments,
not just your expectations.

*It takes tremendous courage
to not admit you were right.*

"
Leadership
is not about
production,
it's about
reproduction.
"

"

There are two types of leaders.

Those who love power

and those who love people.

"

Never trust a leader who wants to be famous.

~

Motives are reversible.
You have the power to choose
and un-choose them.

Even if people
take advantage
of you, stay
generous.

Happy
people never quit,
they just keep
learning.

Your character is measured by your reaction to the unexpected.

A good reputation has nothing to do with your success. It's all about how you've treated people.

Never abandon a friend in their time of need thinking it will reduce your own stress. It will actually have the opposite effect.

Never allow a negative person to be the gatekeeper.

Study the "mover"—
not just the movement.

~

The only way home is forward.

~

Leadership is a constant choice
between character and caricature—
between living the part and
playing the part.

~

Leadership is filled with moods and
moving parts, so just focus on the
mission and stay genuine.

Great leaders empower.
Poor leaders control.

Exaggeration will
cut your influence in half.

Leadership is about stepping toward
the unknown, not the understood.
No leader is ever given the
whole story first.

Stop living suspiciously. Start smiling at people you don't know.

" It's easy to listen
to flattery because

it leaves all the exaggeration up to someone else.

"

Love is not a livelihood. 99% of the people you help in life will never be able to compensate you for it.

Great leaders pay attention.
Poor leaders seek attention.

~

What something looks like initially
is rarely what it looks like
ultimately. So, stay with it.

~

You cannot escape the struggle,
but you can escape the snare.

One of the great tests of the heart
is when someone younger than you
comes up with a better idea.

~

The absence of integrity is
what keeps a gifted person from
becoming an influential leader.

The best leaders are self-aware. Before they walk in a room they ask themselves, "How will my mood affect their mood?"

Ideas are powerful,
but not as powerful as habits.

How you enter the room matters.

A huge part of leadership
is knowing what to ignore
and what not to ignore.

People are
not disposable.
A real leader fights
for the success of
every relationship.

Blocking influence is one of the worst forms of disloyalty.

A big part of leadership
is knowing when to shut up.

~

The next big thing is always
something money can't buy.

~

Even if the good goes undetected,
it will never go unrewarded.
God always sees.

Happiness is never achieved through comparisons. We will always be surrounded by things that are greater or lesser than ourselves in some way.

Work gossip is no different
from church gossip.

~

Emotionally healthy leaders
have two traits:
gratitude for the past and
excitement for the future.

A good leader knows the difference between a gimmick and a game plan.

"

Twenty
years goes
by very quickly
when you're
a leader.

"

It's impossible to moderate
unconditional love. Don't even try.

It's difficult to understand the
value of time until after it's passed, or
the value of money until after it's spent.

It's not your comeback
story alone that inspires people;
it's convincing them they
can make one too.

Keep the vision
adventurous but the
relationships safe.

~

Anyone can be loyal
to a finished product;
it takes real love to stay relationally
engaged to a work in progress.

~

Great leaders notice the positive
before they notice the negative.

The moment someone hears blame in your explanation, they know you're still processing and not yet ready.

The most important thing a leader communicates is warmth, not words.

Not enough right information is just as damaging as too much wrong information.

A great accomplishment cannot compensate for the loss of a lasting relationship.

Even the best version of you still has flaws.

"

Leadership is a
mix of iron and water;
one part is unbending;
the other part is fluid
and adaptive.

"

People get
weary of following
a leader who
talks big but never
follows through. "

There are certain inadequacies embedded into every leader—your God-given shortcomings. They are the gifts that keep you humble and connected.

～

To stay emotionally accurate, you need genuine friendships that have nothing to do with your career.

～

When you serve others, the bitterness from not being served is washed away.

The secret
to high capacity
leadership is knowing
how to turn personal
criticism into personal
improvement.

Be a contributor, not a distraction.

Nothing improves on its own.

Preparation is different from planning.
Planning is about budgets and
calendars—preparation is about
the mind and the heart.

**Most people ask themselves,
"Am I happy?"
Leaders ask themselves,
"Am I authentic?"**

"

The attitude
is always louder
than the answer.

"

A flow chart reveals lines of communication, not the worth of people.

~

There's nothing more dangerous than an articulate fool.

~

Coming across as the smartest person in the room is highly overrated.

Insecurity will emotionally rearrange everything you see and hear as a leader.

It's nearly impossible for two people with pride to reconcile.

Dysfunctional teams spend too much time assigning blame and too little time taking responsibility.

Sometimes all you can do to stop the chaos is build a greenhouse and grow something new.

"
Great leaders know how to maintain

their emotional well-being

in less than perfect conditions.

*The problem
with a bad foundation
is that it can take
years to discover.*

A big part of leadership is
knowing how to make complete
strangers feel at ease.

~

Confidence has more stamina
than enthusiasm.

~

Even if you were born for
something, you still have
to learn how to do it.

The mission of a leader
is to make complex things simple;
it's never to make simple
things complex.

~

Taking responsibility is
different from simply saying
you're sorry.

Loyalty is good.
Blind loyalty
is a disaster.

Never hide your sources.
When you talk about the role others
have played in your success,
people instinctively know you can be trusted.

~

**Criticizing someone
is how the underachiever
compliments himself.**

~

Influencing the decision is different
from coercing the decision.

A good
reputation
is based on two
things: keeping
your promises and
keeping your cool.

People are drawn to a leader who is in relationship with something stronger than themselves.

Hang around
the accomplished,
not the popular.

❀

The anxiety leading
up to the confrontation is always
worse than the actual confrontation.

❀

It's never about your passion alone. It's
more about your capacity to draw out
unscripted passion in others.

"Being missed

is better than
being noticed."

Always keep your heart
twice the size of your brain.

~

What marks a great
leader is not their inability
to offend, but their inability
to be offended.

Even if it lasts a lifetime, it's still temporary.

"

Overstating your significance is just as misguided as understating it.

"

Don't worry about the credit.
People will never forget
who inspired them.

~

*It's impossible to build a team
if nobody enjoys being
around you.*

The best thing about having close friends
is that they can tell when you're faking it.

Nothing is more rewarding than
doing something great for someone and
having it go completely unnoticed.

Discovering your
"ear" is more important
than discovering
your "voice."
Leadership begins
and ends
with listening.

**Don't fear the ordinary.
Some things were never meant
to be one of a kind.**

~

Listening is entirely different
from not talking.

~

**Anything done with sincerity
has the power to grow.**

Love becomes genuine
when it's allocated
toward those who cannot
reciprocate.

" A wise leader can see the bad inside the good, and the good inside the bad. "

Never follow a leader who
isn't following a leader.

You do not move the
unstructured toward structure;
you move the unstructured
toward trust.

Being bold only works if what
you're saying is true.

Good looks
is not where
God looks. His
criteria are what's
in the heart.

Always think long
and hard about
severing a valued
relationship, because
a piece of you will be
leaving with them.

Good leaders make it interesting.
Great leaders make it fascinating.

~

Little gestures move
big mountains.

~

People want to be mentored,
not monitored.

> For an organization to be healthy, the relationships must create more energy than they burn.

The hardest part of leadership
is correcting someone you love.
It's much easier to correct a stranger.

~

It takes rest to run.
It's impossible for an exhausted
leader to stay motivated.

~

A wrong hire is subtraction
by addition.

If you want to waste your day,
spend it chasing notoriety.

**Some of the best learning happens
when there's no place to hide.**

No matter how mundane it gets,
stay relentless about your family.

It takes a lot of
guts to stop a gossip
mid-sentence.

Successful leaders possess two characteristics. They're well-grounded and well-surrounded.

When I compare myself to someone else I always lose my way.

Good leaders speak the truth. Great leaders speak the truth under pressure.

~

The real gift of leadership is making outsiders feel like insiders as fast as possible.

~

The 4 Most Important Questions of Leadership:
(1) *Can I remain honorable when tempted?*
(2) *Can I remain composed when humiliated?*
(3) *Can I remain loving when wounded?*
(4) *Can I remain enthusiastic when corrected?*

Whatever you can't talk about owns you.

You cannot force people to stop feeling something. You can only help them start to feel something new.

A true leader is the one who loves more, not the one who knows more.

~

Procrastination doubles the price of everything.

Don't squander precious energy trying to prove people were wrong about you.

Never collect
your compliments.
Toss them to the
next person as fast
as you can.

Deception never presents
itself as a contrast, it always comes
in the form of a similarity.

Leadership is not about
turning something small into
something big; it's about turning
someone lonely into someone loved.

Building a new relationship is good;
restoring a broken one is better.

"
When someone
takes notice of
your potential,
it's one of the best
days of your life.
"

*What you say matters,
how you say it matters more.*

~

Align yourself with a team
that is talent rich but ego poor.
If you can't find one, then form one.

The fastest way to lose influence is to pout.

"

Welcome them;
don't just
invite them.

"

Integrity means that what you thought, what you said, and what you did are all the same.

Put success on the bottom shelf so anyone can reach for it.

I would rather be in a room full of leaders
than be the only leader in the room.

~

Whether physical or emotional,
you have to cleanse the wound before
you close the wound.

Don't brush aside the person
who has been to hell and back.
You want them on your team,
because they have finally become
the person everyone hoped for.

Coping with uncertainty is much easier when there's an encouraging friend nearby.

~

It's not whether you're outstanding today, but whether or not you're still standing tomorrow.

~

Focus on living— not reliving.

> It's difficult to make progress when your mind is somewhere else.

"
The first goal of leadership is to set standards, not goals.

"

If you need guarantees,
you cannot lead.

~

**Giving up on someone
becomes your loss, not theirs.**

~

It's not what you plant.
It's what you cultivate.

Success has
two inconvenient
demands: getting
started and
finishing well.

Great leaders
see opportunity.
Poor leaders
see opposition.

The only way to become exceptional
is to never see yourself
as the exception.

**No matter how tired, scattered,
or frustrated you become, a great
leader is always in control of what
comes out of their mouth.**

Talking is good. Just pick a
different topic than yourself.

Man adds.
God multiplies.

If the idea was accomplished
by one person, then it wasn't
a big-enough idea.

~

*Whatever you've gone through is to
help those now going through.*

~

Honesty speeds up
the solution.

People who live wide-open and promising bother me—but in a wonderful kind of way.

A smart leader sees potential in the outcast.

Most conflict happens when an under-reaction collides with an over-reaction.

Leadership is not a competition. Never be secretly happy when you see another leader lose their momentum.

The first thing a leader must do is get people to pay attention.

*Productive
people are a mystery to
nonproductive people.*

There's a big difference
between having a meeting and
feeling a connection.

~

*You will never achieve excellence
by living just one notch above the
lowest common denominator.*

~

You cannot threaten
people into loyalty.

Nothing has a
shorter life span than applause.

~

**Behavior does not affect love,
but it does affect trust.**

~

Every time you brag about
yourself, you become
less noticeable.

The moment you admit your mistake, all the necessary components for greatness fall back into place.

Never feel badly for
helping someone remember
their promises. You're actually
helping them remain whole.

~

Listen to the person instead
of trying to read their mind.

Never
downplay
where you've
come from.

It takes courage to tell
a young leader that
you see their gaps,
not just their gifts,
and that you are
equally committed
to both.

The happiest leaders in the world are a
blend of adventure and stability.

No organization has
ever thrived under the leadership
of a control freak.

Destiny is never instant;
that's why a good leader gives
things time to grow.

An effective leader never dismisses
people or opportunities
after one glance.

"

More is always more,

more is never less.

So, think twice before

making new commitments.

Just because you disagree with
someone doesn't mean their actions
should offend you.

∼

Your behaviors are your brand.

∼

You must convince your
conscience of something better,
or the old habits will remain.

Older leaders love legacy; young leaders love destiny. The key is whether or not they can learn to love each other.

> "Leadership is different from management. A manager makes certain the organization is functioning. The leader makes certain it's reaching its full potential."

Popularity is a bad strategy.

The worst kind of selfishness is
self-pity. It takes the energy
out of everyone in the room.

It takes a tremendous amount of
energy to live life avoiding people.

If you can listen to feedback without getting defensive, it will ignite a growth culture throughout your entire organization.

~

Your most important mental skill is the ability to think twice.

~

The best leaders blend strategy with spontaneity.

Even when you're doing
something familiar,
never go through
the motions.

If your only goal is to preserve attendance, then you'll always struggle to speak truthfully.

~

There's nothing wrong with being invisible and laying low. It's good medicine for your leadership soul.

~

Leadership is a combination of your motor and your motive. It takes an equal mix of energy and expertise to become great at what you do.

"

Don't spend the
balance of your life
monitoring the
people who wronged
you years earlier.

"

"

Every time you put yourself down, you take another step backwards and make the journey longer than it needs to be.

"

It's not what you purchase;
it's what you share.

~

Worship God.
Love people.
Manage things.

~

The talent of a great
leader isn't their talent.
It's their ability to spot talent
and collide with it.

Expensive dental work may give you straight teeth and a white smile, but if your tongue tells lies, it was all a waste of money.

Rarely is the wind
at your back at precisely
the moment you need it.
It's usually in your face
making you stronger.

**Not being chosen is
only a crisis if you make it one.**

*Leadership is a tough calling.
It requires coping with uncertainty,
boredom, isolation, negativity, and,
on rare occasions, success.*

**If you gave the gift in hopes of earning
their love, you gave the gift in vain.**

Fast humility cleans up a lot of messes.

Hope believes that what lies ahead
is greater than what lies behind.

~

*Discernment is not the
ability to know right from wrong.
It's the ability to know right
from almost right.*

~

The only thing a leader can impart
to a protégé is their burden.
Gifting comes from above.

The oldest leader in the room
has the ability to bestow blessing
in a way no one else can.

~

Two things mark a great
organization—clarity and charity.

~

People do not respect you because
you've done something great.
They respect you because you've
done something right.

People don't need a persona. They need an actual person who cares about them.

Suspicious people

tend to be lonely people.

You don't have to be ridiculously gifted. You just have to be ridiculously committed.

Living life to the fullest has
nothing to do with power and
indulgence; it has everything to do
with service and moderation.

~

Think twice—speak once.

~

People connect with your struggle
before they connect with your success.

~

When you grow, they grow.

Self-pity destroys a team.
It reduces the well-being of the
whole to the well-being of the one.

It's not what you achieve;
it's what you set in motion.

A clock and a calendar cannot
organize a man's heart.

There is always someone in the room who feels left out; like a mouse without a hole, your job is find them.

Gratitude is the fastest way to
reorganize your emotions.

~

Your job is
to help them up,
not straighten them up.

It's impossible
to build influence
when your primary
purpose is a life of
self-promotion and
self-preservation.

Our world desperately needs its most talented leaders to take on life's toughest assignments.

Delay is God's issue.
Procrastination is my issue.

~

Being your best is entirely
different from trying to be better
than someone else.

~

Secrecy is different
from confidentiality.

~

Be wary of anything that is perfectly
organized and totally successful.

" Good leaders arouse interest. Great leaders build loyalty. "

The servant is the hero,
not the gladiator.

~

*One of the greatest privileges in life
is to help alleviate suffering.*

~

The extra mile is where the treasure lies.

A true leader never stops on a negative.

"

A great communicator can explain familiar things in new ways.

"

Always take time at the end of your
day to think about the kind of day
you are going to have tomorrow.

People will never follow
someone they fear.

If it comes too easily,
it will probably be
forgotten.

Some of the most necessary things for success are located at the bottom of the pit, not at the top of the peak.

~

Hard things make us choose between growth and bitterness. There's no third choice.

~

Revenge actively destroys. Grudge-bearing passively destroys.

Marriage is no ordinary promise.

Screaming at somebody releases nothing.
It only crams more chaos into an already
crowded and confused heart.

~

An average leader Tolerates.
A good leader Celebrates.
A great leader Elevates.

~

The encourager is always the most
memorable person in the room.

~

A leader helps people stay
enthusiastic about the right things.

"
Your three most
important résumé
builders: failure,
fortitude,
and friends.
"

" Fear is a temporary

solution.

You cannot inspire people to live outside the box when you personally lead from inside the circle.

~

The best way to stop thinking about something is to stop talking about it.

~

I've never once looked at a person who asked for advice as weak.

Going first
is entirely
different than
being first.

Discovering something new is good. Rediscovering something lost is better.

Depth determines reach.

~

Gifted leaders do more than confront
people. What they do is draw them
out of the shadows so they
can confront themselves.

~

**No matter how a child starts in life,
the presence of an inspiring mentor
can change everything.**

~

A good leader follows up.
A great leader follows through.

You become a true
change agent
the moment you speak
freely about your own
changes.

The most important
facet of mentoring is connection,
not correction.

*Talk about the things you love and
you'll never be judged as insincere.*

An effective leader knows the
difference between policy and love.

*Be thankful before it
arrives, not after.*

**Don't look for the exit.
Look for the next step.**

~

Failure is refining, not defining.

~

**Always conclude with hope,
even after a confrontation.**

~

The best leaders are those who have a
good relationship between their
mind and their mouth.

You can never fully develop in a safe and predictable environment. It's the surprises that foster strength.

No wound
is incurable—

yours or theirs.”

*If it's deep
in your heart,
then how hard it
is won't matter.*

Branding buys you five seconds; beyond that, it's entirely about content.

~

A flow chart is not a vision.

~

Make the decision with them, not for them.

~

Your humility is more important than your gift.

It's rarely over because you've run
out of time; it's usually over because
you've run out of desire.

~

The reality of leadership is that
you spend as much time pulling weeds
as you do planting flowers.

Somctimcs
a rule tries
to disguise itself
as a truth.
Be careful.

When it comes to vision,
if you are not in over your head,
chances are you're still not in.

~

Never chase respect.
Live an honorable life and
respect will find you.

The moral
to the story
is simple—
don't be immoral.

I've rarely heard something wise spoken harshly.

Two things that are highly
contagious: courtesy and courage.

~

*Being a visionary is good,
but a leader needs to be more of
a doer than a dreamer.*

"
Never compete for the credit; you're just setting the stage for disillusionment.
"

Thoughts and emotions
rarely travel at the same speed.
Sometimes one has
to slow down and wait
for the other to catch up.

The 2 doors

The most beautiful thing in life is opportunity.

When the desire to do something meets the possibility for it to happen, the human heart comes alive.

Opportunity, however, usually presents itself through two vastly different doors. You look through the first door and say, "I can make this opportunity great."

Why?

Because you already possess what it takes to succeed on the other side. In other words, the opportunity needs you.

But when you look through the second door, you see something far different. You see a much greater risk and say to yourself, "I must *become* great in order to succeed."

Always choose the second door.

Through the first door you bring who you already are, but through the second door, you bring the potential of what you must become.